A brutally honest, witty and inspirational anthology of poems and anecdotes giving a heart-warming insight into Alan Oliver's twelve-year battle with terminal prostate cancer.

Written by Alan Oliver
Illustrated by Paul Palmer
Cover and layout design by Matthew Houghton

CONTENTS

ABOUT THE AUTHOR,
ALAN OLIVER (1950 - 20??)

He was born on December 8th. 1950 in the heart of Liverpool, under the name of William Parkes. His birth mother, Anne Parkes, gave him up for adoption at some point, and his new parents, Dorothy and Sydney Oliver, having adopted him around the age of two and a half, clearly found this curly headed little blond bundle too cute to resist. They named him Alan.

Thanks to this wonderful, loving couple, he had, what he describes in his own words, as "the happiest childhood anyone could ever wish for." Dot and Syd, now long deceased, remain forever in his heart as the reason for his fantastic childhood memories, and for making him the person he became.

His schooldays were significant only insomuch as it was a great opportunity to make friends, play sport and generally avoid doing anything too academic. This probably explains why he ended up passing only three O' Levels ... English Language, English Literature and History.

He enjoyed writing verse from a very early age, he was published in the Beano aged about ten, and showed a degree of musical talent, but football and tennis became his obsessions.

He was a popular classmate, being both sporty, and, in his opinion, witty, and would claim to have loved his schooldays if he hadn't had to attend lessons or do homework. Nothing remotely surprising here, and the same could be said of many of his equally distracted, sport and fun loving classmates.

He first went to Goodison Park with his dad to watch Everton in the early sixties, around the time the Beatles were making a big splash on the music scene, and indeed, also a great time for English football generally.

He was fortunate enough to be present at Wembley in May 1966 for both Everton's F.A. Cup Final win over Sheffield Wednesday, and, two months later, for England's only ever World Cup Final victory, over West Germany.

He worked in a variety of jobs including banking, the family travel agency and the local government rent office, but never really wanted to be tied to an office working for others.

So, in 1991 he decided to take the plunge, utilise his verse writing skills, and set up what was to prove to be a highly successful greeting card publishing company, Kamrok Greetings. It was a gamble but it paid off.

Kamrok became renowned for providing the likes of Birthdays and Clintons with best-selling ranges, like Odious Oswald, Molly Coddle and Chuckleberry Pie, for which Alan wrote all the verses, both humour and sentiment.

By now married to Rita, and with two children, Michael and Kate, his business success gave him and his family the opportunity to travel, and for him to indulge in his new-found passion for golf and he was fortunate to be able to play some of the world's top courses. It was also responsible for what has become pretty much an addiction for his kids, and now his grandkids too ... all things Disney.

He got down to a handicap of nine, and by sponsoring himself through Kamrok, funded the purchase of a Variety Club of Great Britain Sunshine Coach for a local special needs school. The keys were handed over by the late comic legend Ken Dodd, and how tickled they all were.

Life seemed to be heading in all the right directions until, in November 2006, at the relatively young age of 55, he got the news that everyone dreads ... he was diagnosed with aggressive and incurable cancer, of the prostate in this case.

Thankfully, his competitive and positive nature played a big part in enabling him to outlive his early prognosis by several years, and he was fortunate enough to see the arrival of four grandchildren … Lily, Heather, Rohan and Harry, over the next nine years.

These kids have been such a blessing to both Rita and him, and have given him even more determination to fight this awful disease. Unfortunately, it now appears that all treatment options have been exhausted, and he and his family have had to face up to the fact that time might be running out.

But even though the outlook may not be great he is trying to remain as upbeat as possible, given the circumstances. Family and friends are playing a key role in helping him "keep his pecker up."

Alan has worked closely with Prostate Cancer UK, who have featured his poems and told his story, to raise awareness of this disease, which kills eleven thousand men every year.

He is hoping that, by sharing his experiences in this book, he will help men to know what to look out for and to get checked if they have any symptoms whatsoever. Unfortunately there can be cases where no obvious symptoms are present, but if there are you will know what to look out for. Please see "The Prostate Poem" in Chapter 7.

He also wants to inspire fellow sufferers, and share his undeniable sense of humour which has helped enormously in getting him, and his family and friends, through what have been some very dark days indeed.

He hopes his journey will give a vivid insight into his ongoing battle with this killer disease, and he has pulled no punches in terms of talking openly and honestly about how he has been affected, not only by his illness, but also by the side effects of his various treatments.

Prostate Cancer UK are supporting this book and will receive a percentage of any profits, which will go towards funding further research, with a view to eradicating prostate cancer as a killer disease within ten years. For more information please visit www.prostatecanceruk.org.

At the time of writing this his struggles continue, but he remains positive because, as he says, "My glass will always be half full, and you just never know what's around the corner."

INTRODUCTION

Okay, I know the title is just about the right side of "Carry On Up the Prostate" (Ooh matron and all that) and to be honest I was going to call this "Laughter ... The Best Medicine" because this book is all about using humour in the fight against cancer and other serious illnesses.

However, and it's a close run thing, I'd probably have to put treatment, specifically and in no particular order, chemotherapy, radiotherapy, medication and surgery at the top of the list. And of course let's not forget the third option and many people's favourite ... alcohol.

We can debate the order of merit 'til the cows come home, but I believe these are the undisputed, glorious triumvirate in terms of getting through the crap ... the Law, Best and Charlton of healing if you will.

The Zippy, Bungle and George of remedies. The Barry, Robin and Maurice of "Staying Alive." Actually, though, that didn't work out for two of them, three if you include Andy.

I actually saw the ghosts of two of the departed Gibb brothers at the end of my bed the other night. Crikey, it didn't half give me the heebee-BeeGees.

Eventually I settled on the title above because whenever I feel beaten up by the whole cancer thing and down in the dumps, which is often, my missus tells me, "Keep your pecker up!" I always respond by saying, "Keep it up? Bloody hell, I can't get it up in the first place!" Read on and you'll see what I mean.

Obviously there is nothing remotely funny about cancer itself. It is a hideous and terrifying disease which devastates lives and tears families apart. I know this from my own experiences, but it is especially true where children and teenagers are concerned, heart-breaking doesn't come close.

Where humour comes into the equation is through the quirkiness of the human soul, and, of course, life's very own banana skins which make us laugh, even at the most inappropriate of times, especially when it's at someone else's expense.

But if you're going to laugh at others, be even more prepared to laugh at yourself. Taking the piss is definitely a two way thing, so by all means dish it out but make sure you can take it too.

I guess cancer affects just about every single person on the planet in some way, either directly or via family members or friends, and we all deal with it differently.

Please don't think for one moment I am belittling the effects cancer has on people, nor that this is a call to arms for all of us "cancer warriors" to fight the enemy.

This is my personal story, and everyone is entitled to deal with scary health issues in their own way. Believe me, any humour or fortitude I have shown, has been interspersed with downright dejection and misery on many occasions. This is no hero's story, just mine.

I was diagnosed with aggressive and incurable prostate cancer in November 2006, and believe me, for my wife, kids and all those close to me, this was no laughing matter. The Sword of Damocles hangs by a precariously delicate thread, especially for those in the grip of life-threatening illnesses.

Having said that, by some miracle and huge dollops of amazing medical care, involving a variety of treatments as listed above, allied to plenty of laughter, a positive outlook, and yes, regular doses of the fourteen percent red med, I am still here.

At the time of writing I haven't yet kicked the bucket (list), however this situation, like my favourite medication, is fluid. As of today, post-Christmas 2018, my clogs have not yet popped.

As a writer by trade, of greeting cards and several humorous books, I decided that it was time to look at this whole cancer business from my own perspective of using humour as a wonderful crutch.

Having a laugh and generally trying to stay upbeat has helped me and my loved ones immensely in dealing with my illness, and that's been one heck of a strong weapon in my personal armoury.

I have worked closely with Prostate Cancer UK and they have featured my story and published a couple of my poems, "The Prostate Poem" and "My Favourite Things," on their social media platforms, which for me is a tremendous endorsement. Especially when I saw the reactions and comments that were posted, saying that my poems had helped someone tremendously, that was very touching indeed.

Anyway, on with the show, and if you are affected by cancer, or any serious illness really, mental or physical, I hope this raises your spirits, gets you smiling and maybe even helps you to deal with all the inevitable crap.

This is not a "Dealing with Cancer Guidebook" because that couldn't realistically exist. But remember what they say the best medicine is ... okay, you win, let's go with alcohol.

1. AN UNWELCOME VISITOR

I first met Mr C about twelve years ago in the Countess of Chester Hospital. I'd heard all about him, about how he was a nasty piece of work who appeared in many guises.

I never wanted to meet him personally, nobody does, but, in most cases we have no choice. He sneaks up on us when we least expect it and comes in, uninvited, hell-bent on causing the maximum damage and suffering.

Thankfully, he often gets his ugly great ass kicked big time by those super-duper medical people, and goes slinking off with his tail between his legs. But even then he can return to finish what he started and exact lethal revenge on those who dared to challenge his awesome might.

He is one powerful enemy, no question, but apart from the amazing array of medical weapons used in battle against him ... the chemo bomb, the radiation laser and the razor-sharp scalpel etc., the thing he hates and fears most is the human spirit, positivity and humour in any form.

So let's give this disgusting piece of shit a huge dose of his most feared enemy ... our own inner strength, determination and courage, allied to huge dollops of laughter as often as possible. Here's my poetic take on that first not so brief encounter.

"MEETING MR C"

Meeting Mr C was a shock to the system
I may have had symptoms but probably missed 'em
He came uninvited, he wormed his way in
And a crap new adventure began to begin

The doctor was forthright, he gave me his answer
"We've done the biopsies, now meet Mr Cancer"
As sentences go, well this wasn't the best
On the day I discovered my unwelcome guest

I kind of suspected this news had been planned
So I said, "Do you mind if I don't shake his hand?"
There won't be a birthday card sent in the post
Cos if he gets his hazardous wishes, I'm toast

That first introduction was truly a stunner
One roll of the dice, Lady Luck did a runner
The bastard snuck in and it's like being tricked
By a toxic intruder so hard to evict

He's cunning and shifty, resilient and smart
And his mission's to stay until death do you part
He's evil, he's deadly, reluctant to leave
But remember, you still have some tricks up your sleeve

So zap him with courage, commitment and humour
Send in the troops, declare war on this tumour
Use all of your strength on this serial offender
Fight on to the end and don't ever surrender

If the spirit is strong though the flesh may be weak
We are millions of miles from being up the creek
We have it within us to conquer his powers
So let's battle this foe until victory is ours.

2. BAD NEWS DAY

Backtracking ever so slightly, the day our fears began to take shape was a Monday, late November back in 2006. I'd been to the doctor's the Friday before due to a prolonged period where I'd had problems passing water.

Truth be told I should have taken my own advice and made that appointment a lot sooner. Don't make that same mistake boys, if in doubt check it out.

The doctor had run a PSA (Prostate Specific Antigen) test from a blood sample, and proceeded to give me a rectal examination. I was hoping he'd give me the thumbs up, however, I'm pretty sure it was just his finger.

His honest opinion was that, like many men over fifty, I simply had an enlarged prostate. Well, that was a relief. He gave me some leaflets with pictures on and told me not to worry. So I didn't, I phoned my wife and told her all was well, I just had a benign enlarged prostate, common as anything. Phew!!!

We really didn't think too much about it that weekend, and got on with our lives in blissful ignorance of what lay just around the corner, on the Monday actually.

The first day of the new week hadn't started too well because I'd had my car clamped in Warrington and needed to get £70.00 in bail to release my poor, innocent vehicle. Never mind, these things happen, so we set off home in our newly-freed prisoner, muttering about the injustices of life.

Looking forward to a nice relaxing evening, and vengeful thoughts of clamping overzealous car park attendants, we arrived back home. And that's when the shit really hit the fan.

There was a message on the phone, I presumed it would be from one of the kids, or possibly friends suggesting a boozy night out. If only! Not in a million years did I expect to hear my GP's rather concerned voice asking me to call him urgently.

Now that tends never to be good news does it. He clearly hadn't called to tell me that my liver showed I wasn't drinking enough booze and to up my intake. Or that I was so fit and healthy I should consider reducing my exercise routine and devouring more Big Macs.

Nervously, I called his number and he informed me that my PSA test showed a reading of one hundred and eighty-nine (normal is from about zero to three or four) and that he had made an appointment for me to see a consultant urologist within a day or so. That in itself was enough to cause a huge lead weight to drop into the pit of my stomach, never mind what was to follow.

Okay, we told ourselves, let's not get carried away. It could be some sort of anomaly, a wonky blood test perhaps, or even some kind of infection. The doctor had actually tried to reassure us that other, less ominous reasons, could be to blame.

But there was a tone in his voice that told me he was trying to stop me pressing the panic button. Deep down I think we both knew what was coming and Cloud Cuckoo Land was not beckoning. The Countess of Chester Hospital was.

So after absorbing this potential bombshell, we decided positive action was called for. Somewhere else was beckoning ... our sanctuary from the woes of the world ... the pub.

"THE PUB"

We wandered lonely in a crowd
And joined the happy, joking hub
Of people drinking, laughing loud
Within our friendly local pub
The setting neither posh nor grand
A fog of smoke, as yet not banned

Our day had gone from bad to worse
The future might be looking bleak
It's something you cannot rehearse
To find you're on a losing streak
Sometimes your problems just seem huge
But comfort was on hand ... vin rouge

We drank, we shared uneasy chat
We said we won't accept defeat
And better out than simply sat
At home with Coronation Street
We contemplated our tomorrows
As we drowned our newfound sorrows

The night wore on, the vino flowed
The room was filled with smoke and laughter
Somehow panic never showed
Though life would change forever after
Years and months, and even seconds
Change when such distraction beckons

The C word hadn't been confirmed
Though our suspicions grew and grew
The doctor's call we later learned
Endorsed what we already knew
As omens clattered in my head
We poured another glass of red

But as the evening neared its end
And, yes, with Merlot fortified
Resolve became our new best friend
"Man up" proclaimed a voice inside
From drowning in the seas of fright
The tide began to turn that night

So if it was the dreaded news
And maybe there was still a chance
Although the message left those clues
We knew the verdict in advance
Okay, accept it, just be strong
And face whatever comes along

The battle lines were clearly drawn
United in our strong desire
Perhaps through wine our courage born
But we would dampen down this fire
We'd fight our foe with punches landing
Twelve rounds gone and I'm still standing

And as we stand here toe to toe
Both bloodied and imbued with scars
There hasn't been a knockout blow
To settle this "dispute" of ours
As both sides put up fierce resistance
This one's sure to go the distance.

3. ANALOGY-ITIS

I love using analogies and metaphors. Why say something boringly, factually correct when you can wrap it up in a lovely, creative analogy? Why travel along the monotonous motorway of mundane madness when you can meander your way along all those winding, wordy country lanes? See, I've just done it again.

For example, my battle with prostate cancer could be likened to a darts match. I'm up against one of the world's most feared opponents, renowned for taking down the opposition and making them feel like it's a total mismatch, a bit like Phil "the Power" Taylor versus Stevie Wonder for example.

Or the New Zealand All Blacks versus the Chelsea Pensioners, not at darts obviously. Or, and I hate saying this, Everton versus Liverpool in the inevitably disastrous Merseyside derby. Disastrous for all Evertonians obviously.

However, giant-killing miracles against all the odds are prolific throughout sporting history and so such powerful adversaries are clearly beatable. They have their weaknesses which can be exploited if you play as a team and get your tactics right.

Oh, and if you have a great manager (consultant), totally committed supporters (friends and family), and a generous slice of amazingly good fortune. All of these were in great evidence in the case of Gary Lineker's favourite Premiership team in 2016.

It's very easy to be daunted by odds, but they didn't prevent Leicester City winning the Premier League then, apparently with odds of 50,000 - 1 stacked against them. Good old Foxes. Basil Brush must've been beside himself, (well he was, literally).

And I can't even begin to imagine what the odds must have been against Mr and Mrs McCallister misplacing their resourceful young son Kevin, not once, but twice, whilst jetting off for their not-quite-complete family holidays. A billion to one maybe? Okay, they were pure fiction, but I suppose it could happen to anyone with fifteen kids or more. Great films by the way.

At this rate of odds defying deeds, and this really is stretching things somewhat, next thing we'll hear is that Tiger Woods has won the Masters for the fifth time. Now that would be something remarkable!

Whatever the odds we face, we could just say that cancer is one total freaking fearful foe, but where's the fun in that? So, in keeping with my obsession with never quite talking in a straight line, and going all around the houses to make a point, here is another little poetic analogy.

It's all about a very nasty train that beckons many of us on-board. It's certainly a far cry from the luxurious experience of the Orient Express, but sadly if this particularly cheerless, chugging choo choo summons you to enter, then enter you must. However, although the ride may be bumpy you have every chance of receiving a Get out of Jail, or Get off This Rail, card.

"THE CANCER EXPRESS"

With plenty of luck, and there's no explanation
The Cancer Express doesn't stop at your station
But sadly for many it can't be ignored
As this cruel locomotive says, "Welcome aboard"

Coming out of the blue, destination unknown
It runs to a timetable all of its own
If you are chosen there's nowhere to hide
And you certainly don't need a ticket to ride

As the Cancer Express rumbles on down the tracks
Many passengers find that it's hard to relax
But please be aware, though the journey is dark
It often slows down, people can disembark

This train might be billowing smoke from its funnel
But often there's light at the end of the tunnel
How things will turn out can be anyone's guess
When you've taken a seat on the Cancer Express

There's no first class carriage, economy beckons
But the odds can be favourable everyone reckons
With hope in your heart and with so much to gain
You can truly expect to be leaving this train

So I'm making this claim, and without hesitation
You need not commute to the terminal station
For with laughter and faith being quite fundamental
With luck your next stop will be "All Clear Central."

Footnote ... It's just a shame that with all the nonsense surrounding the repeatedly appalling performances of Network Rail, the Cancer Express never seems to be affected in any way by unlikely freaks of nature such as autumnal leaves on the line. Now, where on earth do they come from each year, around October?

Actually, train guys, if it helps I do have in my possession a leaf blower. Maybe if enough of us offered to muck in with ours the problems could be alleviated ever so slightly, at least we'd be on the right track.

As for the wrong kind of snow, wet rain and other meteorological phenomena, sorry Network Rail, I'm as stumped as you appear to be.

4. QUALITY OR QUANTITY?

I was due to have my latest consultation with my brilliant consultant oncologist, Dr Azman Ibrahim, at Clatterbridge Cancer Centre on the Wirral. As the local outlet mall, Cheshire Oaks, was en route, I'd arranged to meet my daughter Kate for a quick latte and a catch-up.

We decided to go to the Mafia's favourite coffee shop … Costa Nostra. Actually, the Corleone family don't go there any more since the head of their family decided to Vito it.

As we're sat there talking about her kids, my grandkids, I happened to glance at my watch, aware of my impending appointment. Kate looked at me and asked, in all innocence, "How long have you got dad?"

Yes, it was an open goal, a mere tap-in, but still an opportunity not to be missed. I looked at her, and, in my most serious voice, I replied, "I dunno, love, I'm hoping my oncologist might give me an idea."

A mildly amusing anecdote, certainly, however, it does lead me on to thinking about the whole concept of time and which is most important, quality or quantity?

"TIME"

It's something we wish we had more of
There aren't enough hours in a day
There aren't enough years in a lifetime
Because no-one can keep time at bay
The moments we cherish pass swiftly
The moments we don't seem to linger
But time passes by in the blink of an eye
Or a nonchalant click of the finger
We contemplate life and existence
It's way beyond things we are seeing
We seek but don't find because mostly we're blind
To the rhyme and the reason for being

From the moment we're born the clock's ticking
The egg timer's shifting its sand
Though childhood may seem a perpetual dream
It'll swiftly just slip through your hand
Our schooldays are blurred with confusion
Our teens are a journey of doubt
We all pay the prices of each mid-life crisis
And swiftly approach checking out
If we make it to old age we're lucky
Though some would, I'm sure, disagree
Saying "Truly I'm glad my incontinence pad
Is efficient at soaking up pee!"
So all I can say in conclusion
And I swear it's my genuine belief
Give me one day of pleasure, with moments to treasure
Than a month filled with heartache and grief
Let's live for the day we are living
And however our planets align
We all have a date that's determined by fate
So please, somebody pass me the wine.

5. MY MARVELLOUS MEDICINE

Far be it for me to promote what is after all an addictive drug, but I'm going to anyway. I love my red, red wine, there I've stood up and said it. No, not the UB40 song, that's crap. I refer, of course, to the stuff that used to be made by people trampling grapes into mush with their smelly feet.

I'm not sure I'll be buying Barefoot Merlot any time soon after that thought. "Ah, do I detect the unmistakably distinct bouquet of post fermentation vanilla, subtly infused with the merest hint of smoked almond and perhaps a suggestion of oaky truffle?"

"Well, yes, I'd have to concur with that assessment, however, I'm also getting quite a strong hint of toe nail, athlete's foot and a smidgeon of Daktarin anti-fungal cream." Nice! I guess when you order it with a meal someone has to foot the bill.

Wine has been a good friend to me on the innumerable occasions when that nasty Mr C has got me feeling a little down and in need of a boost. We're not talking glugging it back from dawn to dusk here, just normal social tipples ... yeh, that's what all alcoholics say!

I find it especially relaxing on a balmy summer's evening beneath the hanging wisteria, a faint breeze wafting gently across my fevered brow, soothing and calming as twilight approaches and the stars prepare to charge up their batteries in readiness for their awesome and dazzlingly stellar nocturnal display high up in the ebony skies. This is when I really like to get pissed!

Now, don't get me wrong, I'm not advocating necking a few bottles, although it is a free country. No, just a few nice, mellow Merlots to calm the anxious soul. I am living proof of this because I have outlived all my early prognoses by several years with an unashamed cocktail of prescribed medication along with my regular intakes of the red nectar.

Perhaps it should say on the bottle "take three or four glasses daily" with an appropriate warning about not driving or operating machinery. See, I am a responsible adult. In fact, just to be extra safe, I should add that you can always visit www.drinkaware.co.uk should you feel the need.

Of course, as we all know, it depends entirely upon which day of the week it is as to whether there are any health benefits in the regular consumption of wine. Apparently, on Mondays, Wednesdays and Sundays, throughout the months of April to August inclusive, the damage caused by regular tipples is multiplied significantly.

However, on the other days of the week, particularly from October to the start of January, the benefits of alcohol increase tenfold, peaking on New Year's Eve. Having said that, any day now, a government health spokesperson will appear to tell us that it's all bollocks, and give us a whole new set of boozing parameters and guidelines (or guide wines) to adhere to.

Like most people, I am no paragon of virtue, and I have been known to overdose accidentally on purpose with my fourteen-percent medication. However, I have lived to tell the tale, and believe me, over the years I have had many fine tales to tell.

Even my long-suffering wife Rita, showing steadfast support and self-sacrifice, has always been prepared to join me in my preferred medicinal regime. Same applies to pretty much all of my family and friends, disgraceful bunch or what!

The only downside to this is that, unlike all my other medications and treatments, costing literally thousands of pounds a year, and from which I am thankfully financially exempt, I actually have to fork out for my frequent bottles of Rioja, Malbec or Merlot.

Now these only cost around seven quid a bottle, or sometimes thirty quid for a six pack when Tesco (every little helps) are feeling generous, so why on earth don't these relatively cheap meds qualify to be added on to my prescriptions?

Okay, I'd have to make separate trips to my local street dealer, Appleton Village Pharmacy, as well as my purveyors of the red stuff, but I'd be prepared to do this. Or perhaps pharmacies all over the UK might be granted a licence to provide this essential customer service. Even better.

What a strange world we live in. Anyway, here is my poetic tribute to the amazing medicinal powers of the alcoholic grape juice. Perhaps I should just add that this might not work for everyone, just to cover myself against any potential lawsuits from those poor souls for whom alcohol is a strict no go area.

Also, please be aware of the danger dates as per above, and don't blame me if you get trolleyed on a Thursday in July. I won't be held responsible for the outcome.

"WINE O' CLOCK"

When life kicks you in the goolies, when the shit is all around
When your skies are dark and gloomy
and your mojo can't be found
If your stars no longer twinkle, if you're out of tune and flat
If these and those get up your nose as well as this and that

Don't sit there in bewilderment just staring at the wall
Coz what you will achieve is absolutely bugger all
Stop moping in frustration like you couldn't give a toss
Get off your bum, the time has come
to show the world who's boss

So go and get the corkscrew, we need action, no more talk
Guess what? It's wine o' clock so come on,
pop that bloody cork
Pinot Noirs or Cabernets, cheeky reds or whites
Spumantes or Chiantis, they will put your world to rights

Beaujolais or Chardonnays, or Chateau Neuf du Pape
Some imbued with fine bouquets for when you're feeling crap
Perhaps you'll overdose and start behaving like a plonker
And yes, some of the cheaper stuff
might leave you with a stonker

It really doesn't matter coz your plonk has but one goal
Top of the list to get you pissed and fortify your soul
So trust me, I'm an expert who knows all life's little tricks
Believe me when I tell you there ain't nothing wine can't fix.

6. KEEP YOUR PECKER UP

Unfortunately, it is an inescapable fact that certain drugs, being hormone-based, and which you are likely to be prescribed for prostate cancer, will suppress one's testosterone, which is the rocket fuel behind the male sex drive. Sadly, the consequences are inevitable.

Prostate cancer actually thrives on testosterone, so here's the trade-off … lose some masculinity or lose your life, no brainer really. E.D. (erectile dysfunction) or E.D. (early death). Your call. Unfortunately it can be the equivalent of a life sentence of Brewer's Droop.

The good news is that in many cases this condition can be treated by certain drugs e.g. Viagra, but not always. Sometimes it's a case of Viagra fails and that's certainly no tourist attraction.

I'm not going to shy away from this one because the whole point of this story is about being frank and honest and shirking nothing, no matter how delicate the subject matter.

And, believe me, they don't come a whole lot more delicate than this little doozy. In a nutshell, well, let's just say that without the self-raising agent the cake won't rise to the occasion. "Yes, my dear, if only one could keep one's pecker up!" I think you get my drift.

So the following poem is dedicated to the little trooper who most definitely serves as a member of Oliver's Army. He has been stationed at exotic locations across the globe, has done undercover ops, and it would be fair to say he might not be the most obedient of soldiers.

So, awkward yes, but necessary. So here goes, but first a quickie (stop it) … a friend of mine went to the doctor recently with a triangular erection that had a hint of chocolate and almonds. The doctor explained to him that his body was producing too much testoblerone.

"ODE TO PRIVATE JOHN THOMAS"

Private John Thomas is really a tease
He won't stand to attention, he's always at ease
He's quite insubordinate, bit of a wimp
And he's constantly stroppy and floppy and limp

He won't obey orders whatever the cost
He just hangs around like a little boy lost
His best days are over, they'll never come back
He could be court marshalled, he's facing the sack
(literally!)

Yes, Private John Thomas has run out of gas
He has waved the white flag and surrendered alas
His weapon's not loaded, he's failed in his mission
But he's not to blame for his current condition

Coz sadly this trooper, in spite of his qualms
Had to hold up his hands as he laid down his arms
He put up a fight in his own private way
But was destined to lose at the end of the day

He wasn't a coward, there's no sense of shame
And the court martial duly absolved him from blame
It's all such a pity, however I grumble
That's just how the cookie was destined to crumble

For Private John Thomas it's farewell to action
No longer in service, beyond satisfaction
His purpose in life has been well repositioned
There wasn't an option, he's been decommissioned

But, in spite of his shortcomings, he is a hero
His sacrifice lifted my chances from zero
He showed me such pure, unconditional giving
And he is the reason that I am still living

Against all the odds, he was there to protect
And now he has earned my undying respect
He's held in the absolute highest esteem
Coz my brave little soldier took one for the team.

Footnote ...

This reminds me of the time I was at Chester Zoo and the keeper in the reptile house was explaining about the iguanas' mating ritual. It was quite sad really because, as she pointed out, there was one poor male who was trying like mad, but with no success at all, to make sweet love to his lady friend. Out of the two, she was definitely the calmer chameleon.

The more he tried it on the more frustrated he got, so I asked the keeper what his problem was. She looked me straight in the eye and her deadpan reply was, "Unfortunately, Boy George suffers from ... a reptile dysfunction." I know the feeling little guy.

Guess the poor chap will just have to leave Culture Club and join the Imagine Dragons, cos his chances of a bit of afternoon delight seem to be "Zero." (Title of their song just in case you're not as funky as me.)

Also, whilst on the subject of embarrassing issues I should touch briefly on the delicate matter of incontinence. I have suffered sporadically with this particular curse thus far, so not every day by any means, however it has given me an insight into what really must be a complete nightmare when the condition is extreme.

> *"There was an old man getting sadder*
> *As he slid down the rungs of life's ladder*
> *He wanted to cry*
> *Cos he couldn't stay dry*
> *With his awkward, incontinent bladder!"*

Thankfully there are experts such as incontinence nurses who specialise in helping in these matters, and a quick call to your GP or a visit to Doctor Google will point you in the right direction. This might include booking a flight to the Canary Islands ...Tena-relief?

7. GROW A PAIR, GET CHECKED

Prostate cancer is a plague on the male population, as well as on their wives, brothers, sisters, children, etc. etc. Early detection, as with most cancers, is vital in terms of survival chances, so with this in mind, and with the support of Prostate Cancer UK (PCUK), I wrote "The Prostate Poem" which they kindly published on their social media sites.

The response was amazing. Clearly, the message got through to many people, and, who knows, maybe even helped to save someone's life. Golf Monthly were also kind enough to share this with their readers, including a picture of my flawless, Justin Rose style swing.

Obviously prostate cancer is my specialist subject but there's no doubt whatsoever that early detection of any form of cancer can save lives. We all know that men in particular are loathe to visit their doctor, maybe it's a manly thing. However, Mr C is a bad ass dude and ignore any signs whatsoever of his presence at your peril. Yes, I know, listen who's talking.

We are talking Arnie's Terminator as opposed to Mary Poppins. This is Lethal Weapon and not Bambi. Mr C is no lightweight, like a headache or the common man flu, a couple of paracetamol just won't cut it.

So, get checked, if nothing untoward shows up great. If it does, then you have a fighting chance of conquering this most ruthless and deadly of opponents.

I really hope my poem makes some kind of difference.

"THE PROSTATE POEM"

Guys, listen to me, if you're having a pee
And the flow is just slow coming out
If you're standing there yawning at three in the morning
It's time to remove any doubt
If nocturnal trips produce dribbles and drips
And you feel like a knackered old codger
If the harder you try leaves you wondering why
You're not making a splash with your todger
Well take it from me, you must see your GP
And the sooner the better, don't linger
If your PSA's raised, there's no need to be fazed
But your doctor might probe with his finger
Don't pass on the chance to be dropping your pants
Coz it ain't a big deal, honest, guys
Your awkward full moon will be over quite soon
And it won't bring a tear to your eyes
Boys, the message is clear, you have nothing to fear
And I can't spell it out any plainer
With problems "down there" make your doctor aware
Listen up, it's a total no brainer
So don't be a fool, guys it isn't uncool
Don't be acting all macho and butch
Go on, make those calls, show the world you've got balls
And let's kick the Big C into touch!

8. YOUR HAPPY PLACE

It may surprise those of you who have never witnessed a hospital bay full of cancer patients all tubed up and receiving super-potent intravenous doses of potentially harmful chemotherapy drugs, that seldom could you ever describe these sanctuaries as being in any way, shape or form, places of doom and gloom.

To the contrary, these can often be a hub of laughter and playful banter between patients, their visitors and the nursing staff. Everything possible is done to lighten the mood.

In spite of the obviously serious nature of the business at hand, nearly all those I have spent time with have displayed an optimism, positivity and sense of humour which belies the whole situation. And everyone seems to be interested and care about their fellow patients, which is particularly heart-warming.

An example of humour in the chemo bay (e bay, all treatment delivered online) happened quite recently when I was having a new, stronger chemotherapy treatment. My wife was supposed to be having a girlie day and night out to celebrate her birthday and Christmas.

As this was my first bout of the new treatment, she insisted on staying with me and forgoing her planned outing, not knowing how I would react. Dedication above and beyond the call of duty, though I'd have done the same.

As we were sat there, me all intubated and plastered up, a WhatsApp message came through on Rita's phone and it was a picture of the girls at their hotel in Liverpool, all holding cocktails and raising a glass to us.

Immediately we responded with a picture of me, as described above, smiling and holding a bottle of water with the caption, "Alan's gone out clubbing in St. Helens and he's just having his own cocktail, a Chemo-politan. Cheers!"

As you can imagine, that use of humour, as opposed to "Lucky you lot, out on the razz while we're stuck in here facing a life or death situation!" had exactly the right response and we all had a damned good laugh. Of course the girls knew that we would treat the whole thing in a light-hearted way and they were spot on.

I then added that seeing as I was plastered anyway, I'd be heading off for a nice Indian, with a side of chemo naan. Yes, I know I should be writing jokes for Christmas crackers, but what the heck!

On another occasion, I was being intubated and filled with some nuclear radiation material prior to one of my many bone scans. The poor nurse was having a real problem finding a cooperative vein, and was basically repeatedly stabbing me in the back of my hand in search of a more responsive one.

The poor girl was so apologetic, and she asked, hoping to take my mind off the whole painful procedure, would I like her to put on Smooth FM? Well, it just so happened that Carly Simon's "You're So Vain" came on, so I said to her that this should be called "Your Sore Vein."

Let's say it took the sting out of the situation. Might have been even funnier if the Searchers' "Needles and Pins" had come on.

Later on, after I had started with my first session of chemo and they'd warned me about losing my hair, I let them persuade me to see Shaun (the wig man, honest) with a view to possibly concealing my expected slap head with an appropriate weave.

So I went for my fitting, he sat me in his barber's chair and placed what can only be described as a dead, grey ferret on my head. I didn't know whether to laugh or cry, I looked like Paul McCartney's granddad.

For a moment there I actually thought I'd briefly slipped through the space/time continuum, travelled back to Victorian Britain and turned into Ebenezer Scrooge's jovial mentor, Mr Fezziwig, or, in this, case Mr Fuzzy Wig.

He then started snipping away as if to somehow turn the ferret into something resembling actual hair. At the end of the process, if anything, it appeared to have gained in size, but the guy meant well, I wasn't paying after all, so I said it was a little too warm and could he put it in a bag.

It actually remained in that bag for months, the only exceptions being to entertain visitors, and in that sense it was worth its weight in gold. Eventually, I did the decent thing and returned the ferret to the hospital where I presume it has taken up residence as some kind of mascot, or possibly been relocated upside down, near a tree for birds to nest in. I certainly haven't seen it perched atop any other poor sod's head.

As it happened, I lost very little hair anyway, but if it does all fall out during this current chemo treatment, I can assure you I have a fine array of hats and caps to keep my little head warm. I just might have to ferret around for one or two.

In many ways, this bit sums up the whole purpose of this book, it's pretty self-explanatory. Having said that, we are all human and subject to dark thoughts and moments where the strength of spirit seems in very short supply.

Scary moments can intrude on a million different occasions, so I hope that this gives a little comfort to anyone who is struggling with a life-threatening illness or any kind of troubles in their life and helps shine a little light along the way.

I'm not so deluded as to think for one minute that this little tome is going to completely turn around anyone's misfortune or unhappiness, but if it raises a chuckle or two, I will have achieved my objective.

So this is what inspired me to write the following poem/song, an obvious rip off of the Julie Andrews song from "The Sound of Music." By the way, this was also published on the Prostate Cancer UK social media sites and had an amazing response, I think it went virile (unlike me).

"MY FAVOURITE THINGS"

Thick bacon toasties all smothered in sauces
Playing great golf on spectacular courses
Watching my team, the excitement that brings
These are a few of my favourite things
Quaffing Chianti with friends and relations
Travelling afar to exotic locations
Watching my grandchildren playing on swings
These are a few of my favourite things.

When I'm grumpy
When my prostate
Gets me feeling sad
I simply remember my favourite things
And then I don't feel ... so bad!

Warm apple crumble with lashings of custard
Back to the Future with Marty McBusted?
Getting the box set of Lord of the Rings
These are a few of my favourite things
Watching the sunset and dining al fresco
Buying my Hobnobs with vouchers from Tesco
Feeling the thrill of the first buds of spring
Might even be my most favourite thing.

When I'm frightened
When the chemo
Gets me feeling bad
I simply remember my favourite things
And then I don't feel ... so sad!

Taking the kids off to Disney, Orlando
All Abba songs but especially Fernando
Memories of childhood, the pleasure that brings
One of my absolute favourite things
Praying that one day we will find the answer
How to prevail and eliminate cancer
Life in the future without any strings
We can all dream of our favourite things.

When you're tearful
When you're fearful
When you're unprepared
Just start to remember your favourite things
And then you won't feel ... so scared!

This is my version, but feel free to create your own interpretation of what helps you through hard times, I'm sure it will help. Good suggestions are to think about your favourite time of the year, such as Christmas, birthdays or summer holidays in sunny climes.

You'll have noticed that I've confessed to being an Abba fan. That's fine, I can't actually think of anyone I know who isn't. I guess, if pushed though, I'd have to go for Queen as my absolute top of the pops, with Bohemian Rhapsody as my all-time number one. Saying that, I do have a great old Commodores LP, you can't beat a bit of Vinyl Richie!

I'm actually quite fond of a bit of classical music as well, my favourite composer here has to be the long time "brown bread" German genius ... Beethovis!

By the way, back to the subject of favourite times, somebody recently asked Arnie Schwarzenegger what his best time of the year was and he replied that he ... "Has to love Easter, Baby!"
Yes, I do feel better after that, thank you!

9. THE PASSING OF WIND ACT 2018

Every day, I seem to have a mad half hour or so where my brain metaphorically leaves the tracks and freestyles all over the place, sometimes to places I've never been before. I can one hundred percent assure you that no substance abuse plays any part in this whatsoever, or what follows.

So that's partly the reason, or excuse, for this bit, but to be fair it has earned its place because, as I can testify, certain illnesses and medicines play absolute havoc with the trumpet in your bottom (the bumpet). They can cause it to strike up a deep, not so melodic, solo piece at frequent intervals, however, one normally has the option not to play it.

Unfortunately, in certain situations, the unintentional blowing off of one's brass instrument strikes a rather unpleasant chord. The embarrassment level goes through the roof and as for the accompanying nasal intrusion, I don't need to elaborate.

You could say that with this particular orchestral analogy perhaps I should have opted for an instrument from the wind, or even the whoopee percussion sections. Either way, as you are about to discover, we must all let rip from now on, with no strings whatsoever.

That's just how we must conduct ourselves henceforth and, obviously, the louder the better, or in musical terms ... fartissimo!

Anyway, I really don't think my collection of poems and anecdotes would be complete without reference to everybody's favourite joke material. I have spent over thirty years writing greeting card verses about every subject under the sun (well, almost), and guess what has always proved to be up with the best-sellers? You've guessed it, bodily functions, and particularly botty burps.

If by any chance you happen to be Captain Sensible or even Lord or Lady Intellect, you might want to skip this section and get back to your Financial Times crossword or the next chapter of "Oedipus Rex" by Sophocles. It's a good read, actually, not quite up there with Captain Underpants or Viz, but worth a thumb through. For the rest of you with an extremely well-developed childish streak, please read on.

Now, it just so happens, and I know some of you will be sceptical, but one of the original conditions of Brexit, hitherto unpublicised for obvious reasons, is that from December 2018 it is a statutory requirement for all British citizens to refrain from holding in flatulence, wherever they might be.

This amendment to the constitution was first mooted in parliament before the referendum even took place, but was a heavily guarded secret. Even the Queen was unaware until the actual bill was presented to her one cloudy morning at the Palace of Buckingham. Prince Phillip was apoplectic when he heard the news and almost crashed his Range Rover.

It was proposed by the then Minister for Climate Change, Dwayne Forrest, and his deputy Gaz Greenhouse, and thanks to some unexpected Lab Dim support, helped no doubt by a few G and T's in the Members' Bar, was voted through under the radar so to speak.

The reasoning behind this new bill, apparently, was that members of the public repeatedly holding back little trumps for fear of embarrassment, would ultimately lead to more powerful ones being released into the atmosphere later, adversely affecting the ozone layer and causing polar ice caps to melt.

So, let's assume you are attending an interview for a new job and you feel one welling up inside, you will no longer be permitted to nip it in the butt. Even if you know it will be loud, smelly and exceedingly cringe-worthy, out it must come. Even if it costs you the job regrettably.

I should also mention that this falls directly alongside the Emissions Act of 1965, hitherto pertaining to motor vehicles but later broadened out to include anything or anyone with a noisy and smelly exhaust.

Needless to say, certain executives at certain German auto companies will fudge and cheat regarding the matter of data relating to emissions, from wherever they might originate, but that's for others to debate.

I guess the powers that be figure that if everyone starts losing their trumping inhibitions it will cease to be stigmatised, and become as natural as a cough, a hiccup or a burp, a bottom burp if you will.

Personally, I think the scientific logic behind this sounds like a load of guff, but then probably no more so than most of the nonsense these privileged, pampered old fossils foist upon us at regular intervals.

Anyway, just to be clear, if from now on you are suspected of holding in a fart, you can be arrested, cautioned and fined, or for repeated offenders perhaps a custodial sentence looms at somewhere like Fartmoor (sorry, bad even for me!)

I'm not totally sure how the legal bigwigs will be able to enforce this. I presume they will treat it a bit like drink driving and have the authority to "guffalyse" suspects, or whatever, if they get wind an offence has been committed. And I understand that ignorance of this law will not be accepted in mitigation, so don't say you haven't been warned!

They may even appoint a minister with special powers to oversee this whole process, perhaps a Minister of Guffs, potentially to be nicknamed "the Guffalo?" I'm thinking someone like Lord Skidmark of Staines would be a solid choice to follow through on this.

Look, I totally agree that this all appears to be good news for us medicated to high heaven sickies, we'll no longer have to slam on the brakes when the fartmobile wants to leave the garage. Nobody will care anymore, rather like if we all ran around naked.

Problem is it all sounds like utter nonsense to me and had I been aware, like many duped voters, I might well have chosen to remain and refrain. Anyway, what's done is done so here is my poetic interpretation of the whole thing, with particular emphasis on the actual benefits of breaking wind any time, any place.

And, don't forget, if all else fails and we can't agree a deal, then of course we do have the option of calling a second "Whifferendum." Best of three anyone?

"THE TRUMP LAW,

LATEST AMENDMENT 2018"

Trumps or pumps or botty burps, it's all the same to me
Coz everybody has the need to let the wind blow free
Some are like a summer breeze with neither gust nor force
Innocuous and innocent and odourless, of course

Others may be silent but their potency is vile
The air can be contaminated for a little while
Of course we all deny we've caused that hazy, smelly fog
And if we can we blame our Nan, the baby or the dog

But then there are the killer farts which often follow ale
And they can give a massive reading on the Beaufort scale

They're violent, loud and deadly, tell police if one is near
They'll cordon off the area and keep civilians clear

Well, everybody does it be they president or pauper
Even stars like Taylor Swift, or Pink or … Cindy Lauper
J.F.K. and Ghandi were exponents of the art
And good old Charlie Chaplin did a funny, silent fart

Yankee Boss Man, Donald, having somehow come to power
Is such an ardent fan he has a dedicated tower
And over here in Parliament on any given day
Members pass the bill of farts, who knows, Theresa may

Pep and Jürgen let them off whilst managing their clubs
They'll pop some out whilst nominating who to use as subs
And I guarantee that Claudio Ranieri causes pongs
He may have won the league, but not
without some "Dilly Dongs"

This symphony of wind is universal, played by legions
Some ladies even claim that they can
trump through nether regions
So don't restrain those botty burps,
they're natural and we need 'em
And here's a law we can't ignore, so
give those trumps their freedom

Come on, unclench those buttocks, don't be bashful or discreet
No need to risk imprisonment for a rap you cannot beat
Relax and just let nature do what nature doth endorse
Just do it like Anne Hegerty, "the Governess" of course!

No, don't attempt to hold them back, it's really for the best
Flatulence must never be extinguished or suppressed
You have to lose the stigma, give those farts an easy exit
And if it's tough who gives a stuff?
Just blame it all on Brexit.

Footnote … I actually had a Brexit moment the other day whilst standing at the lettuce counter in Tesco. I didn't know whether to vote leaf or Romaine.

10. IN STITCHES

A few years back, when Prostate Cancer UK told my story and put my Prostate Poem on their social media platforms, they sent a professional team and did a photo shoot of me and my grandkids. The story centred on how, after an initial very bleak prognosis, here was this sixty-something-year-old Grandpa surrounded by those he might never have expected to see.

So there I was, sat on the sofa, reindeer antlers on my head, with my arms around my little darlings. What a lovely, festive scene, encapsulating a loving Grandpa sharing precious moments with his favourite small people. The fact that it was a sunny day in September didn't matter one jot.

We spent hours getting the right images, they had all the gear, there wasn't a Samsung selfie in sight, and it was lots of fun. We all enjoyed the afternoon enormously, especially the feeling of being professional models, and we couldn't wait to see the printed results.

When they came, in the form of PCUK's Christmas appeal newsletter, we were thrilled to see our happy, smiling faces leaping off the pages. It might have been Vogue or Hello magazine, we couldn't have felt more chuffed.

But wait, did my eyes deceive me when I read what was adorning my family, Yuletide portrait? Indeed they did not, for there, clearly printed, were just two words which could have detracted from, or certainly distorted the whole message.

The caption which accompanied this festive, family scene was ... wait for it ... "Never Forgotten." This, in spite of my continuing to be very much alive at that time. Crikey, I'd joined the Dead Poets' Society and didn't even know it!

Now this was of course done in perfect innocence by PCUK, who were most apologetic when I pointed out how people would probably interpret that caption. We had a good old laugh, after all no harm was done to anyone. Well, that's not entirely true.

The moment I chose to show my daughter Kate this rather ambiguous and slightly morbid quote was during the immediate aftermath of her giving birth to Harry, her third child and my second grandson, by means of a caesarean section.

I have little doubt that any ladies who have produced offspring in this way will thoroughly endorse the theory that this is not the best time to be presented with something that will make them laugh profusely.

The combination of simultaneously uncontrollable, hysterical laughter and utterly excruciating pain, was etched upon that poor girl's face, through sweat and tears, to be never forgotten. Just like me really.

The more she screamed in pain, apparently the funnier the whole routine became as she was trapped in a vicious circle of agony and ecstasy. A seemingly endless loop of tortuously conjoined physical extremes, not helped one iota by the reactions of those present.

I must say that, for those of us lucky enough to witness this scene, it was pure comedy gold. Too much to say on a par with Del Boy's uncool fall through the bar, Basil Fawlty's merciless beating of his poor car, Eric Morecambe's playing of the right notes in the wrong order or Father Ted's "racist" rant? Well maybe not, but for pure, unscripted, side-splitting jocularity it was right up there.

By some miracle, no stitches were compromised during the playing out of this spontaneous comedy sketch, and thankfully our Kate can look back and laugh with us, free from the cocktail of mirth and misery she must have endured.

We look forward to the day we can share this story with our little Harry, one day old at the time, and who is now an extremely robust and not so little three-year-old bundle of joy and mischief.

By the way, the hilarity of this entire scenario was enhanced by virtue of our new baby superstar letting off the loudest trump ever heard from a one-day old-bottom. And of course this only magnified the circle of laughter and pain for our poor Kate, it's a miracle she actually survived this episode intact.

The reason I did get to see and hold this brand new farting superstar and my three other grandchildren is in no small part down to the research into prostate cancer which PCUK works tirelessly to fund and support. The facts are that 11,000 men die every year from this disease, and as things stand there are no mandatory checks carried out on gentlemen of middle age and above.

Prostate Cancer UK's aim is to pretty much eradicate this as a killer disease within ten years and I fully expect this to be achieved. Details of how to contact them, either seeking information or offering to support them appear throughout this book, and believe me, this is would be time well spent.

11. PILLS AND POTIONS

Around two years into my cancer treatment, ten years ago now, I faced what I still, to this day, consider my greatest challenge through all of my cancer journey. After a variety of medicines and injections, I was informed by my oncologist that a new drug would be heading my way and that I'd have to learn how to pronounce it.

The name of this medicinal tongue twister was, and it's easy for me to say now ... "Diethylstilbestrol." Okay, your turn. This drug is no longer in service for prostate cancer patients like myself, I guess the doctors couldn't even write it on a prescription.

With pills and potions, apart from their spellings, the thing is that the whole pharmaceutical industry is one big dose of money making trial and error. "Yes, Mr Patient, we're going to try you on this to cure that, however, there is a considerable risk that in the process of curing this and that we may cause irreparable damage to the other." What could possibly go right?

In a way we're all guinea pigs, aren't we? Just read the small print if you dare. Now to be fair, I have been extremely fortunate with pretty much most of what I've been prescribed, hence my continued survival after twelve years, and, believe me, I owe a huge debt to all concerned in the production of my meds.

I offer no magical solutions to this dilemma, obviously there is no panacea to cure all ills, and avoid all side effects. What I can provide, however, is a slightly amusing, maybe ironic little poetic offering which some of you may relate to.

"SIDE EFFECTS"

Side effects, side effects, read the small print
It's written quite small so you may have to squint
With all of your medicines this is the curse
Some are quite trivial but many are worse

From blurring of vision to shortness of breath
You may become faint or experience death
A feast of reactions all waiting for you
But you don't have a choice coz it's catch-22

From fevers to sneezes, from frostbite to sweats
It's no f***in' wonder that some get Tourette's
A dose of the runs or acute constipation
We do what we're told, we're a gullible nation

Some pills give you migraines or cramps in the belly
They make you perspire as your legs turn to jelly
Your head starts to spin, you go weak at the knees
But you just have to suffer to cure your disease

They'll give you thrombosis, they'll clog up a lung
They'll make you feel nauseous, put fur on your tongue
But you're over a barrel, you haven't a voice
Coz the doctors decide and it's just Hobson's choice

They'll make you impotent, you're on a strict ration
By taking these tablets kiss goodbye to passion
So if you're feeling poorly you may have a gripe
When you're faced with that old pharmaceutical hype

A trip to the chemist, prescription in hand
You've just been consulted, examined or scanned
But consider your meds, though you can't expect pity
You may just decide life was best feeling shitty.

12. NO PAIN, NO GAME

Trust me, that's not a misprint. Throughout my twelve-year ongoing battle with prostate cancer, and the previous poem, in all its exaggerated irony, says it all, I haven't really been in what you might call 'unbearable pain' too often.

Okay, there was the time when the cancer had spread quite aggressively to my bones, and there was some very acute discomfort, especially in my hips. Oh, and the time recently when I developed a water infection and it felt like someone was shoving a screwdriver up my willy.

Oh, and when I fractured several ribs falling through the attic by stupidly stepping on the bit between the joists. I don't know what my kids thought was so funny about that. "Stay there dad, we're just going to get the camera and call our friends to come round and laugh at you."

And of course how can I forget the time when I was playing football and, instead of accepting my offered hand at the final whistle, the opposing knob head of a goalie decided to smack me in the face, breaking my jaw in two places.

Yes, that did hurt, especially as I was rendered semi-conscious and thus unable to retaliate. What was worse was spending the next two months with my jaw wired up and surviving on a diet of mushed up food. Thankfully, beer was still on the menu, I just had to be careful not to get so hammered I'd be sick.

Okay, some of these incidents preceded my cancer journey, including the first and only time our kids heard me swear, and I do mean the "f" word. I was trying to disconnect some electric hedge trimmers and, somehow, ended up holding the live wire between my finger and thumb.

I think that near death experience was sufficiently traumatic to justify the expletive, which the entire neighbourhood must have also heard. The patio onto which the sizzling wire fell probably still bears the scorch marks, a permanent reminder of my close encounter with the Grim Reaper.

I digress, so getting back to the cancer, when it had spread to my hips, etc. and that's when I first encountered my current consultant Dr Azman

Ibrahim, at Clatterbridge Cancer Centre on the Wirral. I had been told to expect to be put on chemotherapy, however, he had a magic trick up his sleeve far more impressive than Dynamo could have ever pulled off, hey presto ... Abiraterone!

This wonder drug not only kicked the bone cancer's ass, it gave me about five and a half years of decent quality living. No wonder I called "Abe" my best buddy. Sadly, it has now ceased to be effective and I've been back on the chemo, but I owe so much to those beautiful little capsules.

I was informed from the get-go that they might be ineffective, or only work for a matter of months, but we got on like a house on fire and I miss him like crazy now. When you have a buddy you can totally depend on, entrust with your life, you have something very precious indeed.

Okay, Abe wasn't much into footy talk, or whatever, and he never once stumped up for a pint, but as far as my cancer was concerned, he was my silent assassin. Don't get me wrong, Mr Chemo has been a good mate too, but we do have plenty of moments when we don't get on too well. Sometimes, I'll be honest, he just makes me sick.

But going back several years before all this, I was having great trouble peeing (see the Prostate Poem, guys) and eventually, after being diagnosed with incurable and aggressive prostate cancer, I was sent to have a camera inserted up my wiggly part.

At first, the very thought made my eyes water, I mean I knew it wouldn't be a Box Brownie or a Nikon or anything like that, I'm not stupid, but even a Nokia mobile would surely be a stretch, especially if it started vibrating. And as for that bleedin' tune ... (Did Nokias actually have cameras back then?)

Okay, yes, I'm kidding. Of course it was all done on a tiddly little thing (ooh, you are awful, the camera I mean) on the end of a long wire. Or should I say a cystoscopy using fibre optics, to sound a little less uneducated.

Yes, it was uncomfortable rather than unbearable, but I got to see the inner workings of my old man in glorious, or gory-ous, technicolour. Needless to say, I didn't actually buy the DVD to take home, but apparently it revealed enough to confirm what they suspected.

No spoilers for this eighteen rated movie here, but my ever expanding, cancerous prostate was blocking the passage of urine from my bladder, causing extreme discomfort and taking an eternity to empty the tank. There was only one solution, one man for the job ... calling Captain Turp.

So, who the heck is Captain Turp? Well, surely it's obvious isn't it? T.U.R.P. stands for Trans Urethral Resection of the Prostate, what else could it be? And the Captain is, of course, the highly skilled surgical urologist (medical plumber) who had the dubious honour of drilling a passage down through my willy in order to enable the process of peeing to resume without resistance.

Now this procedure is not one to be done whilst fully conscious, admiring the internal composition of one's urinary tract in perfect wide screen HD, or worse still, 3D. Perish the thought. I can feel my tear ducts welling up as we speak.

In the aftermath of that initial camera inspection, I was going to name the old boy (my manhood that is, not the surgeon) Oscar for his impeccable performance. To be fair, this latest procedure, unobserved by yours truly, thankfully, probably could have been more appropriately nominated for a MOBI award ... Mobi Dick, perhaps?

So anyway, three days spent in hospital, tube inserted "down there" with blood and urine draining off into a bag and a little discomfort, and then it was time to be disconnected, let loose into the big, wide world to put the little tinkler to the test.

Thankfully, after about a week of feeling like I was pissing broken glass, things settled down and the waters flowed freely. The word "relief" doesn't come close to covering the feeling. Mobi Dick became Free Willy. I almost made an acceptance speech, and believe me there definitely would have been tears.

So I dedicate the following piece of poetry to the man, the legend, who gave me back my flow and who saved me hours of occupying men's toilets hoping something meaningful would soon happen. Hang on, that sounds a bit dodgy, I think you know what I mean.

"CAPTAIN TURP"

*"Thanks to Captain TURP I underwent a
procedure called the Trans Urethral Resection
of the Prostate, and it wasn't much fun
But once it was over and I was passing water
normally I was really glad I'd had it done
The Captain wore a surgical mask during
the whole procedure, so I could never
identify him as the operating perp
So all I can say is thanks very much to the masked
superhero who earned my eternal gratitude, the
stranger forever to be known only as Captain TURP."*

Quite recently, and separate to the cancer issue, I was diagnosed with an AKI, acute kidney injury, and admitted to hospital for a week. Part of my package at the Whiston Health Club and Spa involved being treated to another delightful procedure ... a nephrostomy (no, me neither).

Now this basically involved them shoving a long anaesthetised needle into my kidney, not really the spa package I thought I was booking. This was no manicure or pedicure, saying that it turned out not to be much of a kidney cure either.

A couple of days after that delightful experience, I discovered that also included in my package was the fitting of a stent, a short plastic tube connecting my right kidney to my bladder. Apparently, I must have upgraded at some point to a Platinum membership.

Both these procedures, in an endeavour to ensure that clients missed no part of the luxurious pampering procedures, were carried out whilst fully conscious, and if I said it wasn't quite what you'd expect at Champneys, you'd appreciate it ain't on my "things to do again list."

Sadly the fact is that this all has to be repeated around six months later and I am eagerly awaiting my next all-inclusive invitation, literally as we speak.

Anyway, apart from a week's full board, some good laughs with the nurses and fellow patients, and having bloods taken in the middle of the night, I'd probably give them three stars on Trip Advisor and recommend Lenny Henry's favourite hotel chain. My stent in Suite 4B had come to an end.

I'll just share the nurses' favourite Christmas cracker joke ... Where's the worst place in hospital to play hide and seek? ICU. I've heard worse!!!

Deviating slightly for a moment, throughout my life I have had more than my fair share of pain from broken bones playing football, (double jaw fracture, shoulder, three clavicles, ribs galore, big toe etc.) because when I were a lad we played sport, mostly football, outside in all weather. We lived for it and we played to win.

The only time you ever heard the term "Game Boys" was when someone shouted, "We having a game, boys?" Of course we were, jumpers for goalposts and all that. Inevitably our pitch was always a mud bath, think Derby County's old Baseball Ground, and if we didn't come home covered from head to toe in sludge your mum would say, "No game today then?"

You never heard anything sounding remotely like "Nintendo" unless you decided you were in fact going to be Inter Milan's inside right that particular day. Thinking back, we'd actually died and gone to Heaven, and I'd relive that childhood over and over in a heartbeat … apart from school. Okay, school too.

I wouldn't change a single thing about my early years, in the fifties and sixties, and I genuinely believe that the competitive spirit we all developed through sport has come to my aid in fighting this current battle.

Sometimes this competitive streak can be misconstrued as a "win at all costs" mentality, and I do understand this. When I played tennis to quite a decent junior level, I was definitely more McEnroe than Borg, not in terms of ability, obviously, just temperament. I am being serious!

Now it feels like I'm playing either one of them at their peak, or even past it, with my wrong hand and my legs tied together (right, like that would make the slightest difference!). The point being that I'm losing points rapidly and can hear the umpire preparing to announce "Game, set and match …"

The will to avoid defeat is just something you're stuck with, and even now if I play Pie Face or Connect 4 with my grandkids, I want to win, sort of. Certainly, growing up I didn't take kindly to getting beaten and, although I've mellowed over time, I still want to kick this cancer's arse. But you also have to be a realist and accept that you're not superhuman.

So yes, back in those happy, carefree, energetic days we gave it one hundred percent, not a hundred and ten percent which is impossible, and no-one ever hobbled off with a ruptured eyebrow, a dislocated earlobe or, worst of all, a fractured Alice band. No, not Smokie, not that Alice Band.

Young fit players these days on a hundred grand plus per week tired after two games in five days? Fatigue? Rested? Bloody joke. We sometimes played two games a day. Don't get me started.

I must just mention the year 1966, when I was lucky enough, no blessed, to be at Wembley twice. Firstly, to see my beloved Everton win the F.A. Cup, followed two months later by the ultimate sporting thrill of being present as Bobby Moore hoisted the Jules Rimet trophy high above his head before a rapturous crowd which included a certain starry-eyed fifteen year old.

Many years later I played golf with, and got to know, two of that day's heroes, the recently departed Gordon Banks and Sir Roger Hunt. They signed my programme willingly and listened patiently as I wittered on about my memories of that amazing day. Never has the phrase "star struck" been more apt.

Two absolute legends, even if one did score several goals for Liverpool against my Everton, and both couldn't be further removed from the pampered "superstars" of the modern era. And as for Banksy, he played a mean golf game with only one eye, no wonder he thwarted the great Pele with two.

As I said earlier, this whole thing about visualising your cancer as an opponent to be feared, respected and ultimately challenged, has worked for me over the years. Life is full of challenges and there's no doubt this is right up there with the most daunting.

Someone recently gave me a dose of my own analogy medicine, saying, "Actually, I'd compare your current situation to playing match play golf and being three down with three to play!" I thought this was a very good metaphor and responded in kind with "I agree, but don't forget I'm getting extra shots now and I can still take this to sudden death."

I quickly realised what I had said and we both had a damned good laugh. As things stand, now I'm certainly one down with one to play, so not great but anything's possible in this game.

Just a footnote to this, regarding the wonderful game of golf … when you ask someone "How are you?" the almost inevitable gloomy response will be "Well, I've been feeling a bit under par lately!" Here's the thing, it's actually good to be under par, that's the point of the game.

You don't hear commentators saying, "Tiger's been useless today, he's way under par." Just wanted to clear that up. By the way, my favourite golf book has to be "Golf" by A.T. Knowles.

Two other books I'd recommend, and this is totally random, are "Motherhood" by Theresa Kydd and "Security Fences" by Barb Dwyer. Okay, I'll stop!

It's a sad fact that, with any serious, life-threatening or life-changing illness, many of your life's pleasures gradually become stripped away. I have had to face up to this over the years, and now I find myself having to accept certain fun things no longer playing a key role in my life. I won't pretend this is an easy thing to do.

Obviously we've already dealt with a biggie, the physical issue, but I can currently add playing golf and tennis, going to the match, taking nice long walks in the country, going on holidays etc.

All things I once took for granted. Joni Mitchell really got it spot on with her lyric in "Big, Yellow Taxi" ... "Don't it always seem to go, you don't know what you got 'til it's gone ... " Of course, I miss all of these greatly, but what I have found is that the pleasures that remain on your menu expand to fill the void left by those no longer available.

So spending time with family and friends, sharing a joke, watching a great movie, sport on the telly etc. all assume an even greater significance. Even something as simple as just not feeling crap becomes worthy of celebration. I have had to learn to listen to my body and settle for whatever doesn't get me completely knackered. And believe me these days it ain't much.

Thankfully, with four grandkids, that's the perfect antidote for feeling that life is no longer the goodie-laden chocolate box it used to be. But there are still a few hazelnut whirls in there.

So, I try and focus on what I can do rather than the things I can't, but again, I do have days where I struggle with this, especially when the sun is shining and my mates are heading off to the golf course. At least, unlike them, I won't be shooting any triple bogies that day. You've just got to play the hand life deals you, and in my case, be eternally thankful for a lifetime of mostly great memories.

12. FOOD FOR THOUGHT

Unfortunately, and this just goes with the territory, in order to zap those nasty cancer cells, in many cases chemotherapy becomes a necessary evil. I don't need to tell those of you who've experienced it, and I certainly don't want to frighten anyone who may be about to.

The inescapable fact is that chemo is one powerful weapon, however, it carries the risk of collateral damage because it can attack the well-behaved cells as well as the naughty ones and basically leave you feeling like you've gone ten rounds with a grizzly bear.

Fortunately, I haven't reacted too badly to the chemo in the past, but we've had to pull the plug on my latest bout due to some adverse reactions. But trust me it's usually worth the suffering, because at the end there is a great chance you'll have kicked your cancer's butt well and truly into touch. Or, in my case, delayed the inevitable for as long as possible.

And by the way, if like many of us, you have a weight problem, here is a potential bonus, but don't quote me because conversely the steroids they sometimes give to chemo patients can pork you up somewhat as well, temporarily.

So you're probably best taking the following poem with a huge pinch of salt because everyone reacts differently. All I will say is that my own personal weight fluctuation graph has a net variation of about three and a half stone, currently at the very lower end, and my waistline has shrunk to a measly thirty-inches, or six under par. Matalan, here we come again.

Basically, within the space of some four or five months I've gone from being a fat old porker to looking almost anorexic, and my being temporarily (I hope) off the booze hasn't helped matters.

I've discovered bones I never knew existed under all that blubber, quite a shock to the system really. I could probably make a fortune writing a diet book, although whether it would be considered in good taste or not is highly debateable.

I won't be taking on Delia or Nigella any time soon, although strangely I'm hearing Gino de Campo's voice reading out the following poem. And it does have a happy ending.

"THE CHEMO DIET"

So here is a diet, okay it's not great
But it comes with a promise you're bound to lose weight
Once you have started it's just guaranteed
That you will reconsider the ways that you feed
Instead of huge portions you'll just want a bit
But, how can I say this? You might feel like shit
What little you manage to put on your plate
Could soon reappear when you regurgitate
A permanent hangover comes with this plan
And you might spend some time with
your head down the pan
But believe me it's worth it, the hours being sick
You'll get stronger, no longer resembling a stick
So get with the programme, you don't pay a sub
But they only take members of one special club
There's no DVD mixing workouts with songs

No Z-list celebrities prancing in thongs
Just look on the bright side, and think of the fun
That you'll have pigging out once your treatment is done
When food tastes like liver to Hannibal Lecter
And as for the booze, OMG ... freakin' nectar!

Obviously, chemo affects everyone differently and the above is very much based on the expectation of my personal experience of the whole thing and those of a few close friends. In reality, I was luckier than most in terms of all the potentially horrible side effects.

When all's said and done, chemo is the Big Daddy of cancer treatment and if you put your faith in it, and your medical team, you'll have one heck of a chance of beating Mr C.

Stating the obvious, we should all be eternally thankful we have this amazing armoury at our disposal, no matter what our background might be. Our National Health Service and all who work tirelessly within this devoted organisation, deserve our undying thanks, respect and admiration.

14. FRIENDS WILL BE FRIENDS

The whole point, the absolute crux of all of this is that where serious illness is concerned, such as cancer, this is not a battle to fight on your own. Avoid ploughing a lonesome furrow if at all possible.

Quite apart from the amazing array of lethal weapons the medical folks have at their disposal, as well as your own human spirit and strength of will, one more thing is vital.

For the great conflict you now have to face, more than ever you need people around you. A support network of friends, family members, fellow sufferers and even the family pet. It's definitely a case of more is more, build up your own army like I did … Oliver's Army, a frightening brigade indeed. And a motley crew I would add.

I simply cannot put a price on the value of having people there for you, not necessarily breathing down your neck every day, just being at the end of a phone, asking how you're doing and better yet, making you laugh.

But if you are lonely and struggling in this respect then I strongly suggest you contact the likes of Macmillan Cancer Support, Marie Curie Nurses, Breast Cancer Support, Cancer Research or Prostate Cancer UK. Basically, whatever organisation is appropriate for your particular needs.

There are professionally trained people out there waiting for your call. Even the Samaritans if you're really feeling vulnerable and alone. Please make those calls, these people can make such a difference.

I'm very lucky in that I have a large family, as well as a loyal group of close friends, who constantly help us get through all this. So, I'd like to dedicate this poem to all those who've stood beside us when life has taken difficult turns. From my long suffering wife Rita and myself, thanks guys, we love you all and this is for you.

"OLIVER'S ARMY"

When we needed someone in our corner
Just somebody we could rely on
To stand by our side on the bumpiest ride
With a joke or a shoulder to cry on
You provided the strength that we needed
And nothing was too much to ask
When the clouds in our skies threatened tears in our eyes
You were totally up to the task
So the least we can do is say thank you
You have played such impeccable parts
Wherever you go we just want you to know
There's a place for you deep in our hearts
We'll never take all this for granted
It's the most precious gift you could give
All the comfort you've brought, all your love and support
We shall cherish as long as we live
You were there from that first diagnosis
You were there when the outlook seemed bleak
But there wasn't a day when you turned us away

Your devotion was simply unique
There are people who share in the burden
When life takes a turbulent twist
For the deadly disputes, when your army recruits
You were always the first to enlist
The battles, the banter, the laughter
All part of the bitter-sweet years
With people who care and continue to share
In your hopes and your dreams and your fears
You were there when our world seemed to crumble
When our motto was "everything stinks"
And as each little curse grew progressively worse
You were there ... BLOODY HELL, YOU'RE A JINX!!!

Never forget the old saying ... "There's no 'me' in team." Erm ... hang on, "there's no 'I' in united." Well, something like that.

Speaking of Oliver's Army, my first Lieutenant (or more truthfully my Commanding Officer) is without question Rita, my wife of some thirty odd years (not all have been odd, half were even). Through thick and thin really does sum up our time together, but the highs have unquestionably outweighed the lows.

Our theme park ride is definitely more akin to the Rip Ride Rockit at Universal Studios, Orlando, rather than the Tea Cups at Gulliver's World, Warrington, and we wouldn't have had it any other way ... mostly!

With this in mind, several years ago, and just before my cancer diagnosis, I wrote a song called "I Turn to You." Our niece, Gemma Kirby, performed the vocals at Whitby Studios in Ellesmere Port, and I guess it sums up our relationship in terms of how we have always relied so much on each other, whatever challenges life has flung in our direction.

When I wrote this I couldn't have imagined how profound these lyrics would prove to be, so I'm reproducing them here, and, if you would like to hear the song in its entirety, please visit YouTube and search for "I Turn to You, Alan Oliver."

"I TURN TO YOU"

(Words and Music by Alan Oliver)

When nights are restless
And problems come to bear
I know I'll find you there
Right here beside me
When dreams are frightening
Then I can hold you tight
To get me through the night
You always guide me
The moments when this crazy world
Just scares me half to death
I need to feel you close to me
I need to hear your breath

 I turn to you for inspiration
You lift me up so high
And when I need to find direction
Your star light up my sky
You give me faith and I believe in
What you say and what you do
So I get through
I turn to you
I turn to you for my salvation
For answers to my prayers
You are my present and my future
I need you everywhere
Beyond all hope and expectation
My romantic dream came true
So I get through
I turn to you
I turn to you

I turn to you when nights are cold
When I'm afraid of growing old
Everything is crystal clear
As long as I know you are near
I'm mystified, can't comprehend
How destiny sent such a friend
Someone who can understand
Someone who can take my hand

When I imagine
All kinds of scary things
When I start wondering
When I feel restless
I need to know your heart
Is just a beat away
And that is where you'll stay
You leave me breathless
The thunder and the lightning
May come crashing through the storm
But I am not afraid
Because you'll keep me safe and warm

I turn to you for inspiration
You lift me up so high
And when I need to find direction
Your star lights up my sky
You give me faith and I believe in
What you say and what you do
So I get through
I turn to you
I turn to you for my salvation
For answers to my prayers
You are my present and my future
I need you everywhere
Beyond all hope and expectation

My romantic dream came true
So I get through
I turn to you
I turn to you

You are in my life
You are here to stay
Every single night
Each and every day
Now I understand
No matter what I do
Everything is planned
That's why I turn to you

EPILOGUE

I really hope my light-hearted, sometimes irreverent, take on this awful disease has hit the right spot. Perhaps there will be those who find it in "utterly poor taste" and mutter with total disdain, "How very dare he?" But my view is they might have missed the whole point. Either way, everyone has the right to their own opinion.

My own Big C battle has recently reached a critical stage, the cancer has spread quite aggressively and chemo at the Last Chance Saloon appeared to be my only hope for extra time. Unfortunately this particular game plan has been put on hold, for the time being anyway.

It's all very difficult and emotional, especially for my nearest and dearest, but there are so many going through similar scenarios, every single day. It may be a cliché but there really are people going through worse than us, and we never lose sight of that fact.

If the worst happens and the landlord of the Reaper Arms calls "time" as he one day must, I can honestly say it's been an absolute blast and at the ripe old age of sixty-eight, I really can't have too many complaints. The occasional grumble certainly, but few complaints.

I haven't got a bucket list because in all honesty, apart from tobogganing down the side of Mount Fuji on an upturned VW Beetle bonnet, dressed as a Womble, I've pretty much done all I ever set out to. If I did have a bucket list, I'd probably just want to throw up into all of them on a bad day.

"I've lived a life that's full, I've travelled each and every ..." Oh, shut up Frank. I'd rather go out with "Snooker Loopy" echoing around my hexagonal box. I'd take that as my cue to clear my balls off the table, take the long rest and make my biggest ever break. Or maybe there are one or two frames left? Who knows?

I have suggested "How Deep is your Love" might be a good send-off song, well I'm just thinking outside the box while I still can. And I guess anything by the Cure would be asking too much at this stage, although that never really was an option anyway.

Just a word of warning to some of my less than sensitive golfing buddies. I would find this very funny indeed, but I suspect that if any of them, and I mean you John Bickley, standing by my grave, after I'm walking off the eighteenth green for the very last time, started shouting "Get in the hole!" they might not end up invited back to the "do."

Getting back to the footy analogy, (think strong Scouse accent) I'm definitely taking each game as it comes now, to be fair, you know. Yes, I've recently been sick as a parrot, literally, when we've lost a few on the trot, to be fair, but we've had some great results along the way and there have been times we've been over the moon, to be fair, you know.

At the end of the day, the boy chemo done great to be fair, as did my best ever signing, the formidable striker "Abe" Abiraterone who was worth every penny of his huge fee. And who can forget my talented and totally focussed skipper, Captain Turp, who went from one end to the other, keeping things flowing with surgical precision.

There are some tough games ahead but we still have an enthusiastic squad, although one or two are pretty knackered and nearing the end of their careers. We'll definitely just focus on our next fixture and not look too far ahead, to be fair.

Seriously, I can't thank our supporters enough, cheering us along at every game and willing us to win. I'd take extra time in a heartbeat. Wonder what the chances of a replay are?

Maybe VAR will come to my rescue and rule that the cancer should have been sent off with a straight red. Perhaps the ref will award me a penalty in the last minute, if so I'd just blast it and hope for the best. Hey, I can dream.

Speaking of my team, I just want to mention my parents Dot and Syd, long since passed, who very kindly adopted me from an orphanage when I was about two and a half, and rebranded me as Alan Oliver. My birth name was William Parkes, so I guess that makes me Will.I.was. Thanks for the most amazing and happy childhood you can imagine.

Not knowing some of my birth details, i.e. my father, hasn't helped my predicament one iota because the first thing they always ask relating to my disease is regarding any family history. Obviously my own male family members, my son and grandsons, have a huge heads up and know what to look out for when they reach middle age.

I recently sent off my DNA to Ancestry.co.uk hoping to shed some light on my roots. Well I certainly did that, although the results weren't quite what

I was expecting. It appears that a vast chunk of my genes originate in the Soviet Union mostly, the Baltic States and Germany ... only 25% showed as British.

All these years thinking I was a blue, turns out I'm a red. I'm more Vladimir Lenin than John Lennon. Saying that, I'm not about to swap my Scouse heritage for any Soviet roots. "Calm down Comrade!" Who knows, Borat might even be my cousin. The search for my long, lost family continues ... Davina, I need you, but be quick!

With regard to my long found family, huge praise goes to my devoted wife Rita who has shared the burden of all this equally, tolerated my mood swings and quite simply been my rock.

Our exceptional children Michael and Kate and their wonderful partners, Vic and Luke, deserve untold love, admiration and credit for all they have achieved, not least of which being the production of our four grandchildren.

Speaking of whom, Lily, Heather, Rohan and Harry Alan (Master Trump) are quite simply the best gifts we could ever have received. Words cannot explain how adored they are, and they have lifted us to places we didn't even know existed.

Our loyal and irreplaceable friends and family are far too numerous to mention individually. All of you in Oliver's Army have played a massive part in who I've become, so it's your fault really. But I still I love you all dearly, and, as I mentioned earlier, these are now the goodies in my chocolate box of life.

I know I've made many folks cringe thanks to my belief that no joke is too rubbish not to share, you will have gathered that by now. Hopefully, one or two have hit the target and raised a smile, or maybe a laugh. They do say that even a blind squirrel catches the odd acorn.

If my incessant attempts at humour have left some happy memories, it's all been worthwhile. And please, if at all possible, never, ever stop smiling! If I've helped in any way at all, that will be one heck of a legacy to leave behind.

I'm going to sign off with a massive dose of absolute honesty. Through most of this journey into the unknown I've been pretty much able to live what I would call a normal life, i.e. playing sport, socialising, travelling etc. This has made it relatively easy for me to portray someone who, whilst unquestionably having a serious illness, somehow manages to keep a smile on his face and stay positive.

Okay, I've had a myriad of treatments to keep me ticking along, and I've put up with a variety of side effects, some of which I've mentioned. The thing is, now that it's all getting a bit serious and I've turned into an old jalopy with a failed MOT, I'm becoming one big side effect.

Suddenly there is a great big dark cloud hovering above and I'm not going to lie, it's becoming harder to keep up a chirpy front. Sometimes I feel I have to put on a bit of an act, a false, smiley face, because it's what people have come to expect.

The truth is that there are times when I just can't be bothered and I simply want to be a miserable old git whose clock is running down at a rate of knots. Will the real me stand up please.

I mention all of this to simply clarify that I'm as vulnerable as the next person who is struggling to cope with their situation. I'm sure there are many out there, especially children, who are better equipped to deal with the shit that life throws their way, and they all have my undying admiration.

There's no doubt in my mind that kids, especially, are blessed with an inbuilt resilience, courage and just mind boggling grittiness that us old fogies can't even begin to imagine.

And I never lose sight of the fact that I've racked up sixty eight years of living, so, if you ever hear me moan about my lot, please just kick me up the arse.

Don't get me wrong, I genuinely believe that I have dealt with my problems as well as I could have expected, but maybe I should have been more honest and admitted to certain people that life wasn't always as harmonic as I was making it seem.

There are times for everyone when the musical of life hits some bum notes and becomes somewhat out of tune and flat. There again, I guess you'd run the risk of turning folks away if all you ever played were tracks from "Les Miserables!"

I still believe in trying to deal with life's hiccups in a positive way, and with a smile wherever possible, but no-one should feel they have to put on an act just for the benefit of others.

So, tomorrow's another day and, as long as I remain an active, living, breathing participant of the human race, I promise I'll take my own advice and try my damnedest to keep my pecker up.

THE END

"They think it's all over... it isn't yet!"

EXTRA TIME

In the form of one final poetic analogy which sums up my feelings about how I visualise and despise the Big C. I dedicate this to anyone caught up in the whole cancer experience, patients, family, friends etc. It's time to give this piece of work a dose of his own medicine.

"THE SERIAL KILLER"
(CUE COWBOY MUSIC)

There's a serial killer who's wandering free
A nasty old bastard, they call him "Big C"
He rides into town when he isn't expected
And targets his victims, the ones he's selected

Well age doesn't matter, it's their sacrifice
For he hasn't a soul and his heart's made of ice
He chooses at random, the weak or the tough
And attacks with abandon, he can't get enough

The posters with "Wanted" all over the place
Are wasted coz sadly you can't see his face
He's the devil incarnate, an angel of death
Who'll rejoice while we're taking our last dying breath

He's sneaky, he's cunning, he moves like a wraith
And he targets believers and those without faith
The poor and the wealthy, all colours, all creeds
It's his quest to cause chaos, and boy he succeeds

Yes, even our children with lives yet for living
Fall prey to this scumbag who's so unforgiving
Of course he's a coward, perhaps he's insane
Because he gets his thrills causing heartache and pain

A tormenting bully, his name makes us freeze
With no "talent" at all besides spreading disease
He thinks he's protected, completely immune
But I sense that already he's changing his tune

The good guys are totally ready to go
They've sussed out his secrets, revealed his M O
The posse's assembled, good folk, strong and true
So be careful "Big C" coz they're coming for you

He's been causing chaos all over the county
Now the hunter's the hunted, the number one bounty
It's time to turn tables, let's all give a cheer
Let him be the one to experience fear

His days are so numbered, expect an arrest
Coz this worthless assassin is way past his best
He's already spent many years doing time
For repeating each vile, unforgiveable crime

He often transforms into various shapes
Which is how up to now he's pulled off his escapes
But trust me, I'm certain for all that I'm worth
He will be forever despatched from this earth

He is destined to never bring fear to our town
I believe absolutely this scum's going down
He will be destroyed, every person survives
So good riddance to this monster that devastates lives.

"It is now!"

THE END

ACKNOWLEDGEMENTS

My editorial team, John and Lauren Bickley

My graphic design team led by Matt at MH Designs

My illustrator, Paul Palmer

Everyone connected in any way to keeping me alive long
enough to write this, including you Mr. Merlot.
Contact me at: alanolly1@outlook.com

DEDICATIONS

I dedicate this to Oliver's Army, which comprises ... my beautiful family,
especially my unbelievably courageous wife, Rita, our children Michael
and Kate and their partners Vic and Luke, and of course our four gorgeous
grandchildren, Lily, Heather, Rohan and Harry.

To all our extended family and our network of loyal friends, all of whom
have given their unbending support.

To Doctor Ibrahim and his team at Clatterbridge Cancer Centre on the
Wirral, who've kept me going longer than I could ever have expected.

And to Prostate Cancer UK with whom I have worked closely to help raise
awareness of this indiscriminate killer of men. Through their amazing
efforts of raising money for research, I have no doubt that they will
achieve their target of eradicating prostate cancer as a death sentence
within a decade.

All of you have given me the love, inspiration, and most of all, a reason to
fight this thing with all my power. Words could never adequately express
my feelings towards you all. Thank you!

Printed in Great Britain
by Amazon